HEALTH

TAKE CARE FOR HEALTH

JIGYASA SHUKLA

Made with ❤ on the Notion Press Platform
www.notionpress.com

I thank myself for this idea.

Contents

Preface

I like to write new stories made by me

Acknowledgements

The Acknowledgments section is where you recognize and thank everyone who helped you with your book. It's a way to display your appreciation to them in a public and permanent forum

Prologue

A prologue or prolog (from Greek πρόλογος prólogos, from πρό pró, "before" and λόγος lógos, "word") is an opening to a story that establishes the context and gives background details, often some earlier story that ties into the main one, and other miscellaneous information.

CHAPTER ONE

NEHA WENT TO DOCTOR

A girl name Neha who was 11 years old. She did not take care of her health. She always ate junk food like; pizza, burger, chowmin, cake etc. Her elder always advised her not to eat junk food. Her mother said her Neha, why are you not taking care of your heath? Pizza, burger, chowmin, cake these are not good for your health. It will affect you badly one day. But Neha did not listen to her mother. After few month Neha fell ill. Her mother took her to doctor. Doctor asked to test the haemoglobin of Neha and her mother tested Neha's haemoglobin. When report came it showed Neha surfing in anaemia and her haemoglobin is 7. Doctor prescribed Neha to eat fruits and vegetables, drink milk and juice, gave her some iron tablets and after that her mother talked to her again, I always advised you to eat heathy food but you never listened to anything. If you had listened and ate healthy food you would not have been suffering from anaemia. Then Neha said sorry! And promised that she will eat healthy food. After 3 months when again she went for blood test, there was improvement in her health and haemoglobin as well. And from that day Neha a healthy lifestyle and food.

Name Jigyasa Shukla

CHAPTER TWO

OBESITY ATTACK

Ranjan a very rich man his son name was sikhander.
His father and mother always busy in thier work.
Sikhander lived with his grandmother.

Because of old age his grandmother was always not able to make food for him.

Hence Sikhandar used to eat outside.

Most of the time he ate pizza, burger, chowmin, etc.

Day by day he become fat One day he went to the health doctor

Health doctor check his weight , it was 75. Doctor calculate his BMI

The result was over weight and obesity

Doctor prescribed him to stop eating junkfood and doing exercise daily to loose his weight.

From that day Sikhander stop eating junkfood and eat healthy fruit, he starts erercise daily

After eight months he went to doctor and check his weight. It was 65, he had lose 10kg in 8 months

now his BMI was normal. He became happy and thanks to the doctor and promise him that he will never eat junk food more and do exercise daily.

How To Take Care Of Health

1) Eat a healthy, balanced diet with lots of vegetables and fruit.

2) Keep your immunizations up-to-date.

3) Don't use tobacco, vape products, alcohol, or drugs.

4) Exercise as often as you can.

5) Stay aware of your emotions and moods.

6) Get enough sleep.

7) Wear proper protection at home, work, or play

What Are 8 Ways To Stay Healthy

Measure and Watch Your Weight.

Limit Unhealthy Foods and Eat Healthy Meals.

Take Multivitamin Supplements.

Drink Water and Stay Hydrated, and Limit Sugared Beverages.

Exercise Regularly and Be Physically Active.

Reduce Sitting and Screen Time.

Get Enough Good Sleep.

Go Easy on Alcohol and Stay Sober